TEN POETS

Martin Appleby

Dawn Vincent

James Domestic

Amy Wragg

Leon The Poet

Mary Fucking Poppins

Ricci Read

Ricky Frost

Tonkabell

Jackie Montague

Published by Earth Island Books

Pickforde Lodge

Pickforde Lane

Ticehurst

East Sussex

TN5 7BN

www.earthislandbooks.com

Copyright remains with the authors

First published by Earth Island Books 2024

Cover design by James Domestic

Front cover photo by Tom Blackwell

No part of this publication may be reproduced, distributed or transmitted by any means, electronic, mechanical, photocopying, or otherwise without written permission from the author.

ISBN 9781916864184

Printed and bound by Solopress, Southend

Contents

MARTIN APPLEBY — *07*

Don't Look Them in the Eye — *08*

If You Don't Dress the Wounds of the Past, Then You Continue to Bleed — *10*

Street Fighter — *11*

Don't Try — *12*

That'll Show 'Em! — *13*

Gentrify Me, Baby! — *14*

DAWN VINCENT — *15*

Eulogy For The Living — *16*

Skin Pickings — *18*

I Am Here On Purpose — *20*

Al Dente — *21*

Replaceable — *23*

The Living Stone of Your Skull — *24*

JAMES DOMESTIC — *25*

BBC — *26*

Best Before — *30*

Don't Call It "Winter Blues" — *32*

You Should Be Happy — *34*

AMY WRAGG — 35

Poetry Is — 36
Willard Wigan — 39
The Noble Amateur — 40
I Won't Tell You Who To Vote For — 43

LEON THE POET — 45

The Happiest Man in All the Land — 46
The Number 1 Father of the Year — 49
My Last Song, A Drunk Woman, and a Cajon — 51

MARY FUCKING POPPINS — 57

Dots on the Train — 58
Strategic Abandonment — 59
A Sick Bucket of Red Flags — 61
Magic Alleyways — 63
Modern Kids, Crumbling Futures — 64
Shit Sandwiches — 65

RICCI READ — 67

Welcome — 68
Renewed — 70
Method & Madness — 73
Pollution — 76

RICKY FROST — 79

Stage Name	80
Even When There is No Weight	82
Did You Know?	83
Postmortem	86
Patience in Petals	88

TONKABELL — *91*

Snake Oil Salesman	92
Tie A Yellow Ribbon Round My Fucking Mental Health	93
Reign Down on Me	94
Everyone's Shame	96
My Anxiety Made Me a Spliff	97
Under the Rubble	98
I'm Queer	100
They Brought Me Flowers	101

JACKIE MONTAGUE — **103**

Act 1: The Love Test	104
Bethnal Green Girl	107
Dirty Weekend Dream	109
A Sitcum	110

Martin Appleby is a punk, poet, vegetarian, cider drinking scumbag from Hastings, England.

He edits Paper and Ink Literary Zine and runs Scumbag Press.

Website: scumbagpress.co.uk

DON'T LOOK THEM IN THE EYE

I seldom notice

peoples' eye colour

I could not tell you

my wife's

nor could I tell you

with 100% confidence

my own

But what I do notice

is that people

who pay attention to

such things

are often the same people

who squeeze too hard

when they shake your hand

The same people

with little to no regard

for personal space

the same people

whose voices are permanently

several decibels louder

than necessary

The same people

for whom it is requisite

to be the centre of attention

at all times

And further

I notice that there is often

a direct correlation

between an overbearing desire to

exude confidence

and a lack of personality

That is not to say that

the limp wristed

anxiety ridden

whom won't look you in the eye

cannot be equally

as dull as their handshake

But I would much rather

spend time

in the company of

the latter.

IF YOU DON'T DRESS THE WOUNDS OF THE PAST
THEN YOU CONTINUE TO BLEED

You can say any old shit

as long as it fits in to a pithy phrase

and people will believe it

as long as it sounds prophetic

then people will repeat it

they'll share it on social media

in a fancy typeface

over photos of lakes or forests or mountains

they'll tattoo it upon themselves

they'll live by it

and die by it

then engrave it on their tombstones

People are idiots.

STREET FIGHTER

"*What are you studying?*"

a girl asked me

it was my first week of university

and I was at a Freshers party

"*Screenwriting*" I replied

"*STREET FIGHTING?!*" she exclaimed

I laughed, before correcting her

but she was much less excited

by the actual answer.

DON'T TRY

Two words
emblazoned on Bukowski's headstone
under the image of a boxer's silhouette

A tattoo on my right arm
in Courier New font
next to the logo of my literary mag

It is a call to action -
if you want to be a writer
write

It is also apathy -
why bother?
in four billion years the sun will explode
and none of this will matter

It is also a warning - a threat
fuck around and find out

However you read it
whatever you take from it
it is one hell of an epitaph.

THAT'LL SHOW 'EM!

I read that when actor Matthew Perry

first appeared on the cover of People Magazine

he sent a copy to one of his old teachers

that had told him

he wouldn't amount to anything

if he messed around all the time

I wish I could remember the names

of any of my own former teachers that disliked me -

I would send them a copy of this poem

in whatever chapbook / zine / lit mag / anthology

 or obscure literary blog that it appears in

None of which I will have made any money from

and, in fact, if I have published them myself

then it will have cost me money

for them to be able to read it

That'll show 'em!

GENTRIFY ME, BABY!

Gentrification is bad
I know, I know
I get it -

Rich folk moving in
bringing their fancy cafes
and boutique shops

Raising rent prices and
forcing lower income
people and businesses out

Gentrification is bad
I know, I know
but hear me out -

My local greasy spoon
does not have any
non-dairy milk alternative

And the only vegan option
on the entire menu
is dry toast.

Dawn Vincent (she/they) lives in Colchester, performs at spoken word events and is running poetry writing workshops in 2024. Dawn has a self-published novel and collection available on Amazon, and a memoir of her experience of being bullied available on Kindle and Spotify as a free "pod book". Dawn is passionate about sharing their experiences to help others.

Dawn loves to travel to eat in new places and wants to visit every Disneyland Park in the world. She has never managed to follow a recipe to the letter and her favourite stories and experiences are ones where life has gone off-map.

You can follow Dawn on Instagram at @dawnislosingtheplot for more news, poems, and updates and a high chance of photos of her dog.

EULOGY FOR THE LIVING

You were never sure how to do this
and, part time,
you did fine
I guess
by 90's standards.

Inadvertently taught me how to:
avoid food poisoning,
to stuff fistfuls of 20ps
from the pub till into the Minstrels machine
to keep tummies from rumbling
and boredom hitting
when the football took over the sky dish
(though it was entertaining
to interrupt it
with silly games).

You checked out when we were teens
and since then
I have parented you
more than you ever have me
despite me being
no longer your obligation.

You were never going to be a meet-for-cake Dad,

an I'm proud of you Dad,

a sleeve rolled up and helping with the house Dad,

shared wisdom Dad, none of that.

I'll focus on what we did have: memories;

some horrific, some fine, some ok,

and all the lessons

you didn't mean to teach us

tucked away for another day.

SKIN PICKINGS

My skin is knitting back together
after I pulled and bit it apart
again.
it must get angry that I ruin its work
fuck up its faultless seams
again.

Sigh, resigned, when I get a new cut or scab or bruise
and feel the rush of something new to abuse.
It will try to heal faster than I can poison the wound
and it will try to save me from myself,
sting to stop the dirt in the new layers of skin
and I will smile back in defiance
and say:
I like it that way
I like the pain
I'm going to do it
again.

At night, the fight stops
I surrender for 8 hours if I'm lucky
and my arms are still
so this body wearily pulls some strings
pieces me together

knits flesh new
like a mother tired of sewing up knee holes
in school trousers.

And yet I'll do this again
take this miracle of healing for granted,
just presume my body will put up with this
as long as I decide to put it through it
again.

I AM HERE ON PURPOSE

After Vanessa Kissule's 'Come Over Here'

Nothing says 'I mean to live'
like getting on with it –
making plans,
despite my brain's complications.

I love you deliberately
and that, too is an act of faith
that I'm sticking around
and I intend to, not just for now.

Those words were hard-earned
and saying them feels like confirmation
that I am a long, long way off
leaving this land. I am here on purpose.

AL DENTE

You are going to find your ingredients first:

A dollop of bickering in IKEA.
A pint of compromise.
Mystery - not sure where from.

Years together,
shared memories
knowing each other like
you know your own skin
and somehow
it's still fun;
you're still in love.

Agree that you both
prefer your pasta
slightly overdone, smothered with cheese
and piled high.

Do not serve; share.
An Alexa to ask in a rush
if you can share it with the dog
even though it's still too hot.

Have time apart, come back with stories.

Method:

Bake, box some up for lunch, then plate it.
For dessert, raid the fridge
for chocolate you were saving
for a special occasion.

Do not serve; share.

REPLACEABLE

One among us leaves
and we spread thinner to fill the gap
like crooked teeth
just to save a millionaire some cash.
I am disposable.

They will spit me out with blood
and smile
with a closed mouth
to hide the rot
in the gaps
where the pearly whites
chipped to nothing
and left roots.

THE LIVING STONE OF YOUR SKULL

After The Cryptonaturalist aka Jarod K Anderson

It's a delicacy to eat the brains of duck and fish,
scoop or suck their tender tissue out.
I'd like to think I am more than meat
but to be honest,
underneath the animated fossil of my skeleton –
I am just overactive flesh talking crap.

Despite that,
if you hold your hand here
you will feel a hum;
that is the beating ocean of my heart.

Run your fingers over the cliffs of my ribs,
rock pools of blood and fleshy creatures
under the skin - some proof of life.
One day it will all crumble into nothing
and that's fine with me
but for now, I am here, present, sentient,
so alive I can taste it.

James Domestic grew up in Essex, is a compulsive songwriter, a musician, DJ, painter, poet, and punk.

He's toured the world and elsewhere with The Domestics and made records with more bands than is healthy or sensible. He currently resides in Suffolk.

At the time of writing, he has two illustrated volumes of poetry – 'Domesticated' Vols.1 and 2 – published by Earth Island Books, and another, co-authored collection (with Dave Cullern), called 'Cruor'.

www.earthislandbooks.com

www.jamesdomestic.com

For live bookings email jamesdomestic@hotmail.com

BBC

BBC
BBC
when I think of all the things
you've given to me
well, not given
but purchased
through the licence fee
to see you now
makes me bawl and weep
from a broadcast hero
to a puppet for creeps
I can't in good conscience
and in all honesty
really think of you as the BBC

You're like a friend
whose awful behaviour
I can no longer defend
who'll step in to save you?
edging closer to the line
over time
spitting at the line
kicking at the line
moving the line

erasing the line
then trying to tell us
there never was any line
and if we did think that
then we're simply victims
of some communist plot
that sold us a lie
about some fictional line

Please don't let your baby see
the BBC
it'll alter its brain fundamentally
and most likely hobble
just one of its feet
so it'll lean to the right
for eternity

You lie, BBC
you lie
by tone and omission you lie
it's no longer like decades ago
when almost everything
that you'd know
came from a scant few sources
and set parameters
for our discourses

Information

Entertainment

Education

those are the core tenets

of your mission statement

along with public interest

and impartiality

so have you got amnesia, BBC?

Now, it's not my intention

to regale you

with rose-tinted TV nostalgia

but your independence

once a source of pride

has in recent years

been compromised

Many of us are all too aware

of the stories you choose

to *not* put on air

footage of mass demonstrations

ignored by the nation's station

of camera angles avoided

and deceitful footage alloyed with

scripts that are skewed

truths mangled and chewed

and a country more firmly divided

Language is important
at the end of the day
and at the start of the day too
and it's not just what you say
but how you say it
and what you choose not to say or do

Whenever you mention
striking workers
the implication's
that they're greedy shirkers
you conspicuously omit
any other grievances
the conditions, recruitment
and staff retainment bits
and it's never a surprise
'cos it's every bloody time
Someone's setting your agenda
but it's not me or mine

So, BBC
it's getting harder to see
just what kind of service
You're providing for me
when the trust has gone
and it's gone on too long
it's a
British
Broadcasting
Con

BEST BEFORE

His 'Best Before' was 2004
now it's 2023
the 'Use By' date is a different matter
it's like an official reprieve

Beyond the 'Use By' is a judgement call
it's kind of discretionary
but if there's fluff, or clicks, or a funny ol' smell
I'm afraid you're beyond warrantee

He was lying awake on a Tuesday night
too troubled to get off to sleep
he knew his best days were behind him
and he glanced at his missus, Eileen

Still a great beauty in his eyes
and they were a thirty year team
any day now she'd check on his dates
and boot him out into the street

But just as despair squeezed him tightly
a memory hoved into view
Eileen was six weeks older than him
so she was half-knackered too

A wave of relief swept all through him
he dabbed his damp eyes with a tissue
those 42 days were his saving grace
and she was unlikely to raise the issue

DON'T CALL IT "WINTER BLUES"

I have the supposed magic lamp
but no wishes are granted
I changed the bulbs in every room
but I remain half-hearted
a spray of max strength vitamin D
for my former self; supplanted
the GP put me on Sertraline
but still I'm disenchanted

Please don't call it "winter blues"
not if you know what's good for you
that makes it sound like a minor ailment
when it's a portion of mental derailment
that you must
chew
and chew
and chew
and chew
until there's nothing left of you

Shrinking back inside my husk
recoiling from perpetual dusk
fogging up my frontal lobe
my faculties have now eloped

anxiety at every juncture
your sense of self is winter-punctured
and autumn has you in a fugue
your chemicals are eating you
chew
and chew
and chew
and chew
Until there's nothing left of you

I have the supposed magic lamp
but no wishes are granted
I changed the bulbs in every room
but I remain half-hearted
a spray of max strength vitamin D
for my former self; supplanted
at least four months of every year
it's like my brain has sharted

YOU SHOULD BE HAPPY

I don't think I'm gonna make it
look at the state I'm in
I'm on a raft of medication
and a boatload of vitamins

I feel it in my body
and I feel it in my mind
I won't reach a ripe old age
I'm running short on time

I'm always trying to create things
that will go on after me
and I'm haunted by the suspicion
that I'm never gonna be

Happy in my surroundings
and comfortable in my skin
truly happy in all the ways
you should be happy in

Amy Wragg has been running gigs in East Anglia under the name of getonthesoapbox since 2006. Based in Ipswich, Amy has been writing and performing her own poetry for over a decade. She also loves covering her favourite poems at the monthly SoapBox spoken word open mic, Words & Verses, which she hosts. Word Nerds unite.

Photo by George Fairbairn.

#getonthesoapbox

www.getonthesoapbox.co.uk

Insta www.instagram/getonthesoapbox

POETRY IS

Poetry is time travel.
Poetry is preservation.
Poetry is at a funeral pleading the case for
reincarnation.
Poetry is political. Poetry is personal.
Poetry is a public performance ritual.
Poetry is quiet and whispers in your ear.

Poetry is kindness, and anger, and fear.
Poetry is forgiveness. Poetry is prayer.
Poetry is hogging all the toys and refuses to share.
Poetry is filthy and sexy and rude,
but poetry considers themselves to be a prude.
Poetry doesn't agree with you.

Poetry is revolution!
Poetry is just fine.
Poetry is child with a magnifying glass
in the garden for the first time.
Poetry is pointless.
Poetry is mostly written at night.
Poetry is a rabbit caught in headlights.

Poetry is humble. Poetry likes to bimble.
Poetry volunteers at the local library
Every saturday morning
but poetry can't stop yawning.
Poetry is a bad dream
nights sweats, and sleep walking.
Poetry is important.

Poetry is beauty, poetry is bold.
Poetry doesn't need anyone
and won't do what it's told.
Poetry is a boy. Poetry is a girl.
Poetry prefers non-gender specific pronouns
and refers to themselves in the third person.
Poetry is desertion.

Poetry is your granny's trifle.
Poetry can be found at midday holding a loaded rifle
insulting your mother.
Poetry is undercover.

Poetry is melancholy.
Poetry is receiving counselling
and has been prescribed antidepressants.
Poetry is an obsession.

Poetry is patriarchy.

Poetry is at a party and has drunk all the beer.

Poetry is always near.

Poetry has been stalking you on facebook

and looking at all your holiday pics.

Poetry is a prick.

Poetry had a dream

and now it's not sure if it's real any more.

Poetry is sleeping on the floor.

Poetry is duty. Poetry is cruelty.

Poetry is a letter to an ex they're never going to read.

Poetry is a disease.

Poetry is a feeling everyone has but cannot express.

Poetry. Is. Under. Duress.

WILLARD WIGAN

He paints
in between heartbeats
in a hollowed out hair.

He worries
that the paint may dry
before it reaches the surface.

He sculpts
crowns on the head of a pin,
camels on the horizon, and
a universe in the eye of a needle.

'Oh, it's gone.
I think I might have inhaled it.'

THE NOBLE AMATEUR

(Dedicated to the great poetry wars of 2018)

An amateur poet is the right kind for me
writing lyrics & lines about life and what is seen.
It's accessible and honest,
and I like it that way.
Universal truth spoken aloud
in the language of the day.

Ranting & raving, maybe
fucking swear like there's no tomorrow.
We'll effectively use social media
and from pop culture we'll borrow.
We don't know the rules,
or we do but don't care.
It's not technical or highbrow
and it's making some people scared.

Young, popular and talented,
but not a member of the 'proper' poetry crowd.
How about we form our own club?
Where everyone is allowed.
Anyone who loves words
and language, that's all that's required.
(Though we do like to have fun with it
so a sense of humour is desired.)

Writing for the 'great unwashed',
once said about the Liverpool Poets,
& they knew what it was about then
& now we're the poets that know it.
Poetry can be ridiculous (see above)
and funny and silly.
Written badly on a bus
it might even contain willies!

The rhyme scheme is basic
& the words aren't academic,
but that doesn't mean I'm stupid,
this is the way I want to say it.
And what's wrong with clarity?
And personality? And emotion in art?
When I seek out inspiration
I want someone who speaks to my heart.

So I say 'hooray' to all the amateurs
speaking words on the mic.
Writing exactly what they want to,
without worrying if its 'right'.
To the professionals I say:
'be kind to each other,
don't hold poetry so tight
it eventually gets smothered.'

Maybe I'll never release a collection,
or maybe my books will outsell yours,
but please don't be bitter cos
Hollie McNish is in all the bookstores.
Poetry is a broad church
with room for all kinds of people,
with different styles & approaches,
no hierarchies, we are all equal.

We live on the same street.
We're neighbours, let's try to be friends.
But Watts does need to accept,
no one gets to decide where poetry ends.

I WON'T TELL YOU WHO TO VOTE FOR

I won't tell you who to vote for
but I will plead with you to vote

Yes I know it can seem pointless
and they might all sound the same
and the media churns out stories
that fill your heart with doubt
but don't be fooled by apathy.
Please believe your vote does count.

I won't tell you who to vote for
but I will tell you what I'm voting against.

No privatisation of the NHS
a slow dismantlement of
the best thing this country has ever done.
Free healthcare for all.
Life's worth not measured by income.

I won't tell you who to vote for
but I will tell you what I'm voting for
I'm voting for radical change
the protection of all worker's rights
a fairer tax system that charges
those who can afford it
just a little bit more, cos surely that's right.

I won't tell you who to vote for
but I will plead with you to vote

Tell you all about my husband
who stood in the 2019 election
a paper candidate they said
you really don't have a chance
Imagine our surprise when he won,
genuinely by a margin of 'one'.

I won't tell you who to vote for
but I will tell you what I'm voting against

Against this idea this country should fear
the other, the migrant, the refugee
the demonization of people,
we're all just people,
I hope one day they'll all see.

I won't tell you who to vote for
but I will tell you how to vote

Vote with optimism
Vote with hope
Vote with love in your heart
Vote for the many, not the few
Vote for each other.
Vote for you.

Leon The Poet is a writer/podcaster/performance poet and musician. Leon's poetry is sometimes funny, often bleak, occasionally personal, and political. What he strives for is authenticity and honesty. He is just as likely to be found penning wry observations about the social minutiae of life in a soft play area, as he is writing about cult mind control.

Leon presents the A Hug from The Moon podcast, which you can find on Spotify etc., and you can follow him on Instagram @a_hug_from_the_moon_

THE HAPPIEST MAN IN ALL THE LAND

The man at the bus stop
Is the happiest man in all the land
one hand on hip
a smile on his lip

His legs twisted together
like an Office World Mick Jagger

And to top it all off
a mid 80s
Magnum P.I moustache

He had an itch
between his arse cheeks
and you know what?
He itched it

He didn't give a shit
he just did it

The most self-assured
happiest man in all the land
he couldn't wait to get on the bus
pay for his ticket

and sit down
and watch the faces and the trees and all the
outside blur into one giant abstract
impressionistic scene

He went home to his one bed flat
said 'Hi honey I'm home!'
and fully laughed out loud
because he lived alone

He sat in an upright purple single seater armchair
and watched 80s reruns of classic TV
The Sweeney
Minder
Beadle's About
Cagney and Lacey

He sat in stained white undies
and a pimply barely-there chest
with paunchy delightful belly
that sat there like a beige jelly

He fizzed open a can of weak as piss lager
and fed himself wafer thin ham

When he ran out of beer and ham
he left the detritus where it fell
cos 'what the hell?'

He stumbled to bed at 11 o'clock.
on a mattress with no sheet
he collapsed face first
and broke his nose

He woke up the next day
with a fizzing popping thudding in his brain
and a face and a chest
and a mattress
full of maroon stains

And thought...
'I can't wait to do it all again.'

THE NUMBER 1 FATHER OF THE YEAR

The macho dad at the school gates
is like the Great Wall of China
I can see him from space
hear him coming, see him bowling
bawling out his boy for something
and he points and laughs at his penis
must have seen it earlier and remembered
how small it was
the boy's shoulders crumple
like an empty peanut packet
this dad sure does make a racket
if I wasn't such a coward I'd go up to him
and karate kick him in the chin
the crane technique from the karate kid
and someone would shout 'finish him'
and the macho dad
would have a friend behind him yelling
'Yeah, Johnny put him in a body bag!'
and laugh like he's never heard a joke in his life

The bell goes and the macho dad pulls his kid close
'Come here!', 2 slaps on the back
pushes him away
just in case anyone watching thinks he's gay

and he's on his way
bowling with the strut and swagger of man who's
never found a feeling he couldn't laugh at
pummel, or slyly take the piss out of

Meanwhile his boy has met his best mate in school
the one he's got secret crush on
later on, they'll get called gay
and the boy will pummel that thought away
along with his best friends' face
and dad will laugh when he hears about it
he'll boast of it at the school gates and call the kid gay
he'll square up to the best friend's dad
and in his confused face he'll see weakness
he'll pummel him too
and pop it in with the rest of his war stories
and compare cuts on his knuckles with his sons
and feel like he's number 1
the number 1 father of the year
undefeated

MY LAST SONG, A DRUNK WOMAN AND A CAJON

I'm playing in a pub
on a sleepy summery Sunday
most punters supping pints in the garden
and getting lairy
and I'm last on the bill
headlining I tell myself

But it's the worst spot
because everyone's half cut
or gone home early to sleep it off
cos it's a Sunday
and there's only so much happiness you can
borrow from Monday

The bar is sparse
like church on cup final day
five people including the bar staff
I do my songs and I don't say much
between songs
and I shut my eyes as I sing along

A dog walks in
and he gets more fuss than me
upstaged by a bloody border collie

I race through my songs
pleased to be nearing towards the finish
and as I can see the finishing line in sight
I get a little cocky, a little giddy
and before my cover of Olly Murs
I tell the story of how
my sister went on a date with him
and how my dad now randomly hates him

And how my other sister
once went to a Burger King with Coolio
and wouldn't you know
I get a titter and a giggle
from somewhere in the middle

Onstage there is a cajon
the guy who runs it
nice guy
name of Jason
sometimes jumps on there and pounds out
a perfect beat
as a treat
to accompany the singers before me
but right now he's nowhere to be seen

And as I near my final song
one which was written specifically to singalong
ironic considering I'm playing to an empty bar
competing with the roar of a broken pint glass
a drunk woman sidles over
and sets herself up on the cajon
aits like a cat
straddling a nuclear bomb

And I say
with all the confrontational skills
of a mid-90s Hugh Grant

"Erm, can you play that?"

"No but I'll give it a go"
she slurs
with all the gaiety of a well-oiled lady

In that moment I face a choice to pout or preen
have a tantrum
just come clean
"Love, you're not playing with me.
Go on, Sling your bingo wings
And get back to your pitcher of gin
cos just in case you're wondering,
I do care about sounding ok
and this isn't a jam night "

But I don't say that

I look into the crowd

and into the eyes of her other half

and his dead eyes seem to say

best get this over with me mate

So, I count her in

and would you believe it something amazing

happens as I play my song

we start to get in time

our eyes lock and we are in perfect sync and rhyme

we blaze through the song

the crowd goes wild

And the crowd carry me aloft

and I get drenched in half pints of mild

And the drunk woman?

We are now a 2 piece

getting all the big gigs

in cut price Premier inns

across the country

So, the moral to the story is

don't leave a cajon unattended on a stage

and never be too afraid to say

"'Piss off, I'm playing a song here"

otherwise, you might just find yourself

playing the 02

with a drunk 60-year-old named Pru

Mary Fucking Poppins is a Scouser published in numerous places such as Paper & Ink Zine, Late Britain zine, and with a chapbook out with Backroom Poetry.

Mary produces Word Vomit Zine and poetry open mics at Round The Corner, Liverpool.

https://www.instagram.com/word.vomitzine

https://backroompoetry.sumupstore.com

https://strictlyunprofessional.bigcartel.com

Email: punkpoetry@protonmail.com

DOTS ON THE TRAIN

He gets on the train
I'm not actually sure if he is in fact a he
or if he could be a she
which is sound
cuz that's never bothered me
the long brown hair down to the knee
is nearly sat on ever so neatly
nothing like me, pinned to the seat
in pranging public transport anxiety
my eyes now super glued to my feet
I count the dots on the pattern
in the train seat Infront of me
their cough
pleasant sounding in the open door
contained by closed palm
I continue to count the dots
while the train announcer counts the stops.
1 more till I get off
sadly they got off on the one before.
leaving through the automatic door
and probably never to be seen again
now just a window reflection memory
disappearing
in large loosely fastened shoes.

STRATEGIC ABANDONMENT

The Iron Lady scrounger
tory Prime Sinister
through the years of 79 to 90
pondered a lethal procedure
An injection of managed decline
with its dirty syringe set on Liverpool city
following the united unrest
of the Toxteth's riots.

So, a filthy fallacy of managed decline
was sadly suggested
The mangey ministers argued
not to spend any public penny
on the stoney ground of Merseyside

Chancellor Howe spat that it would be like
trying to make water flow uphill
as we are famously a hard nut to crack
which was made ever so graciously evident
during the general strike of 1911
the year everything stopped in Liverpool

The trains, railways, factories and ferries
the docks and dockers

shops and shoppers

in all towns both sides of the River Mersey

all came together to tackle the tournament

of their ornate Tory oppressors

who were dishing out low wages and

and unethical working conditions

leading to living in squalor and squat

But that summer of resistance reluctantly ended

when a frigate war ship was summoned

down the River Mersey from the south

Ordered to train its guns on Liverpool

to discourage our lefty united anarchy

from igniting in other cities in the country

I ask is it not at this point we should have

sent them to The Hague?

and get rid of this Tory plague

once and for all

A SICK BUCKET OF RED FLAGS

If they hide their toothbrush

It's possibly a red flag

If they can't ask for what they want with words

then it's probably a reg flag

If they talk to you via any other form of

communication, such as a suggestive look

a fast movement or a slamming door

this could all be a juicy red flag

If they have a mirror on the dashboard

of their car or van

red flag

and they probably take a lot of speed

If the car they drive

is not registered in their name

A royal red flag

If they claim to be great at pulling out

deffo a red flag

and they are likely to have tadpoles in many pools

and plan to put one in yours

If they are always looking for post

but never pay bills

it's probably a red flag

If they act like a bad man

then they probably are an annoying cunt
which is a red flag
If they try to poke holes in you while you're "asleep"
deffo a red flag

If your shit starts going missing for no good reason
then it's a red flag
If you see your PlayStation and electric drum kit
in the window at the Cash Converters by your house
it's a fucking red flag
and they also probably have pay day loans
in your name

If you can't listen to a certain song
without wanting to scratch the disk and your eyes out
that's a red flag

Trust your gut
and believe your eyes
when the red flags fly

MAGIC ALLEYWAYS

I love alleyways
it's where I've done all my best wees
it's where I find all the best treats
like furniture
scrap wood for the bonfire
and other boss freebies

I love it
when the students all move out
and we end up with a practically brand new
couch and a TV wall mount

My best days have been spent
in many magic alleyways
I can't wait to find a new place
with some decent outdoor space

All in good time
but for now
there's plenty of decent alleyways
around by mine.

MODERN KIDS, CRUMBLING FUTURES

Kids these days
barely surviving a tainted age
after merely managing a pandemic plague

A maze of no mercy
the longest drought of democracy
fairness Lost in a deliberate daze
free school gruel only dished out
in southern posh postcodes
what a dystopian dire strait

Bambi's dodging danger
around every corrupt corner
weans raised in disorder.
A candid, vivid childhood for many
lost in a synthetic glaze
mirroring sorry and sad traits
lost in debates and crumbling walls
a severe selfish sabotage

SHIT SANDWICHES

A Shit sandwich Is unplugging your bath
to a knock on the door
to say your neighbours ceiling is leaking
and failing in
but it's slightly bearable
because it's now Wednesday morning
and there is a new episode
of the Blindboy Podcast

A shit sandwich is
finally putting enough gas on your gas card
so not to have to worry about
whether to wash your hair or your dishes
but now you can't use either
until your plumbing is fixed.

A shit sandwich is
losing a partner, but gaining a friend

A shit sandwich is losing your mind
but finding a pen

A shit sandwich is having no money
but having your own space to breathe
even if the air inside it is cold.

A shit sandwich is toasted

with a full pot of tea

but you fell asleep

and now it's stewed

and both near froze.

Ricci Read is a poet based in Colchester, Essex. He aims to capture the complex human experience of love and loss, hope and despair, whilst mixing in existential philosophy, beauty of nature, imagination, and trauma, as well as his own autistic and mental health experiences.

Ricci has one book under his belt (at the time of this publication) called Earth Man. You can find details of this book and more of his art on his Instagram @riccireadart or website riccireadart.bandcamp.com

Ricci is one half of the Poetry at Events team alongside his wife Billie. They host a regular night in Colchester called Poetry at Patch. Go to facebook.com/poetryatevents for more info or email poetryatevents@outlook.com

WELCOME

(The purpose of creativity is connection, I hope we
can form an understanding of each other)

Stretching out my hand to you,
tearing through this book.
I long for connection; Bait, Line, and Hook

Sharing poetry is vulnerable,
these pages hold my heart.
blood is now on your hands.
please use it as paint
when creating your own art.

I long to inspire and to be inspired.

Speaking to strangers,
I have so many questions to ask.
coming together,
building an ark.

The floods are coming.
The floods are here.

Read my poems

and know my fears.

know my joy,

hold my tears.

Thank you for your time,

whether minutes or years

RENEWED

(This poem speaks on depression and suicide. I
 present an opposite of Sylvia Plath's 'Tulips'. Instead
 of a reluctant return to life, I am desperate for it.)

Give me Sylvia's flowers.
bring me back to life
with petals of perpetual pain.

(Duhkha) life: suffer, change.
rain dancing in the eternal moment,
petrichor peace.
flooded heart,
anchored deep.

Bring me those tulips.
their persistence & patience
against Plath's reluctant optimism
and my own longing.

Arm me with angelic armour,
a halo for a Helmet.

I have filed my horns down to their nerves.
Torrential torment.

Stay dancing in that rain,
may we bloom again.
Allow me to wear my mind
as a crown of roses.
My body has long been the thorns.

My dreams attack me,
waking up from hellish realms.
My ambitions planned suicide.
My hands recoiled from themselves.

I had to dig my way out
with bone exposed fingertips
through planets of dirt.

Free me.
Snake shed this sickened skin,
let light win.

This sadness is shackled in,
to a Maddened mind.
Drag it all back like sand
through the sea's tide.

Stand there, knee high,
drowned under horizons.

Glittery diamonds,

the soul adorned in sunrise.

A new day,

renewed.

METHOD & MADNESS

(A deep longing for understanding and purpose but always pulled back by confusion and loss).

I set sail
across a sea that never longed for me.

I thought I dreamt the salt on my lips,
maybe it was a memory
of another's ambition.

What had made me sweat,
in the cold fever of hope?
What made me think that I could remember,
once I had awoke?

I do not know…

Maybe it's the sky that I chase
or the fleeting moment itself.
Either way,
the waves are ravenous and unforgiving.
Still
Strong experience beckons passion from within
Aching deep inside my skin.

Trying to again join the wind.
Stirring morning
Reconnecting
Resonating
Resurrecting

My coffee sometimes contains all of life
inside its crushed beans
and tastes the flavour of love.

Like it's the last drink I will ever savour.

As if the beautiful calm birds
that I watch through my window may turn on me,
rip my eyes out and eat me whole.

Repeated eternity,
similar to Prometheus' fate
but that's a sinking thought.

For nothing is eternal
but energy
in this breathing multiverse.

I contain energy and no soul.
Stardust seeking home.

Awareness strapped to bone,
oxymoronic oxygen
with each breath
taking me closer to death.

Zigzagging from epiphanies to confusion,
spiralling intertwined with truth and illusion.

There's method and there's madness.
The two cocktail together on this treacherous trail;
across the sea, where I set sail.

POLLUTION

(A glimpse at the horrors of capitalism and industry)

Black smoke in blue sky,
my blue eyes watch and describe
as it turns to grey blankets that we lie in.
As we're lying to ourselves,
comfort in dying.

Infinite chimney smog.
The laugh of no god
fills our lungs
as it distils, dilutes and shoots the air
with its prescribed pills.

A world of addicts, saying they're not killing themselves,
but they're dying.
we are all dying.

"Last warning for
Global warming!"

Most like their poison
in teaspoons,

as not to face the facts.
Others run cold baths
to slit their wrists in
and lie back.

Some are fighting, good for them.
Maybe it is too late.

From doomsday preppers
to due dates,
earth rotates
one great grave
with no escape.

At least it can feel that way.

It sure can feel that way.

Ricky Frost is a spoken word artist and poet from Essex.

Growing up in a household with ignorance towards mental health issues, he found solace in writing. It became a tool for self-expression and reflection.

His writing explores a variety of topics related to mental health, including stigma, recovery, self-care and how important it is to look after each other.

https://www.instagram.com/rickyfrostpoetry

STAGE NAME

Have you ever lied about something
so often, you begin to fool yourself?
Living with a nickname is no different.
Eventually it just sticks.

I have a nickname I hear every day.
I call it my stage name,
for I can be consumed by my costume.
I am a contortionist of sorts,
you'll see only what I want you to see.
Hear me laugh like an avalanche,
gathering my impressions,
rehearsing every word.

We, the performers,
the social transformers
we have this innate ability
to animate our pain;
a smiling wide kind of ferocity,
a glass half full philosophy.
Confidence is a performance,
and comedy is just confetti.

If I give you a nickname, an alias, an AKA
I'm imploring you to share this stage,
to improvise an elaborate disguise.
I find it harder to blend in the background
when I'm the only one around
so when I'm feeling down,
I surround myself with a crowd
and quietly take a bow.

EVEN WHEN THERE IS NO WEIGHT

When planning out the foundation of a house,
the architect must think of everything.

He must consider every possible outcome,
every worst case scenario.
He must account for the maximum weight,
for he knows stress can cause
even the sturdiest structures to collapse.

What are we if not architects
of our own mental health?
I am constantly reviewing my blueprints,
even when there is no weight.

Don't wait for the worst case scenario.
Don't wait for the weight to be too much.

DID YOU KNOW?

As a kid, Little Brother was inspired
by the weird and wonderful.
Sci-fi storylines, conspiracies,
wacky facts, that sort of thing.
I'm the eldest boy, once top of my class.
I thought I knew better than everyone else,
but I remember the first time
Little Brother proved me wrong.

He wanted to bet me
that it was possible to time travel.
Had me like "*I got this in the bag.*"
Did you know at The Geographic South Pole
holes are poked in the logic of time zones?
A step forward can take you an hour ahead.
One step back an hour behind,
the hands of time moving alongside you.

I have learnt a lot from Little Brother over the years.
Did you know the Earth has seen more trees
than our galaxy has held stars?
Did you know there are sentry geese
in the Chinese police force?
Did you know that when dragonflies mate,
they create a little heart shape?

"We could go to New Zealand"
he once said, out of nowhere,
"Did you know, that's the furthest we can go
before we start coming back."
The day Little Brother decided to end his life
he called me to apologise.
He'd swallowed some pills
that would send him to sleep.
It was his style to be sorry
for something he couldn't control.
He'd always had someone else's sadness in his hands.

Statistically, annually around 800,000 lives
are lost to suicide.
How do I explain
that he is more than just a number on a page,
more than data on a bookmark saved.

Do you have any idea how to forgive someone
when they're not at fault, or what to say
when a phone line sounds like footsteps fading?
Did you know that the brain can be a cassette tape?
Memories replayed will not feel the same.
Rewind to an 80's tune or Mum's perfume.
Forgotten fields and alleyways.
Every hurtful name I ever gave.

Did you know

there's an hourglass buried in your chest?

Every beat is a grain of sand

slipping through your hands.

This happened a few years ago,

or maybe a month or so.

There is no time zone that would let me let this go.

I thought we were too late but he came through

to prove me wrong once again.

Little Brother; I have also made mosaics

from memories. No matter how far apart

we are, if you've got anything to say,

I'm only a phone line away.

POSTMORTEM

We'd been apart for a couple months, maybe three.
A room at capacity yet she was all I could see.
She didn't look this way, but I know she spotted me.
She had never taken my breath away like this,
never had I felt this nervous around her.
A love once strong now had me writhing inside,
unable to look each other in the eye.
It felt worse than any fight we'd had.

The next day I sent a text.
I said I know you're my ex
and these things often become a mess
but can we clear the air?
We've been pretending not to care
yet we both know that we used to.
I said let's meet for coffee.

We met on a Friday at three.
We acknowledged we were
worried about acting awkwardly
and then we simply talked.

She listened to me between sips of tea,
She didn't argue, didn't disagree.
She spoke considerately,

and I didn't argue, I didn't disagree.
Two surgeons immersing.
With gentle words, we took turns
to dissect the murder of us.

We dismembered the body to recall everything else.
We determined cause of death
and accepted what was left.

Love makes no promise to last forever.
It's just a point of view, a perspective we can't choose.
When we lose, it doesn't mean it was any less true.

And indeed, we lost our direction,
we fell from each other's orbit,
and that's normal, but that day, that half hour latte
we chose to remember the rotation.
It was a simple postmortem
performed from a love that once was.
An autopsy of the moved on.

PATIENCE IN PETALS

As a teenager I would have made a terrible gardener.
I was far too impatient. I had those knee grazed days,
that fast paced, fists raised phase.

I had an urgency to be all guns blazing;
I chose to ignore every warning sign,
like the snarl before a rabid dog's bite.

I just felt angry all the time.
Anger is just misplaced patience.
It's a passionate hastiness, proving the wrong point,
It's poisoning pollen
prohibiting the promise of petals.

Now, patience is the most powerful tool I could
possibly use, I've sown hope and grown composure.
This perennial persistence keeps me
looking for the garden in every graveyard.

There is no collective noun for a group of gardeners.
Perhaps this is because patience is something
we need to learn on our own.

I pursue the payment of patience;
I picture clouds like a watering can,
the sky has a foolproof plan
and I shall not interrupt it.

I think of those that love me just for being me.
A love given without reason other than
the wish for me to grow.

If I prune, I'll bloom. Every day I'll be someone new.

Tonkabell is a Manchester-based poet, who writes poetry about politics, eyeballs, serious issues and wanking.

They maintain their right to spell most things incorrectly, as they are a proud dyslexic and an even bigger knob head.

https://www.instagram.com/tonka.bell131

SNAKE OIL SALESMAN

there's a snake oil salesman on the loose
who quite absurd , who quite obtuse
who trying to sell their magic beans
and trying to make a massive scene
the salesman deals in foolish gold
he'll fool you into his control
his carpet isn't really magic
his reality is so awfully tragic
he's mutton dressed as sexy lamb
he doesn't care or give a damn
he'll find you at your lowest point
without a beer without a joint
his reputation come in waves
his heart is burried in a grave
avoid the snake who tries to sing
coz luck ain't what he's guna bring

TIE A YELLOW RIBBON ROUND MY FUCKING MENTAL HEALTH

tie a yellow ribbon round my fucking mental health
it's been several long years
since i found it on the shelf
my mind is twisted up and my brain is inside out
please please make it stop, i always scream and shout
the voices in my head lack sympathy and kind
my way out of this labyrinth i doubt I'll ever find
my brain breaks into pieces my sanity's a must
nothings making any sense and life is so unjust
noise and noise and noise
just running through my head
what did you just tell me
what have you just said
it takes a toll on life, it cuts my heart to ribbons
my psyche collapses once again, as i am not forgiven
something's wrong with process
and something's way too dark
nothing feels like anything, and love is always stark
things do seldom matter, the news will never shock
lies are scattered everywhere and seem to run amok

REIGN DOWN ON ME

Its 5am, water rains down my window
It drips softly on the roof tiles
I look outside to my concrete jungle
And see new buildings for miles
My bed is warm, my windows intact
My coffee pot makes me a fresh brew
I shower in hot water and dress
And skip off to see my crew
Dogs run round the park all day
People smile amongst the grime
In my cloudy Mancunian dream
Nothing is running out of time
The transport bustles on its way
Taking people everywhere
The homeless man sleeps wherever
And no one seems to care

Its 6am, bullets reign down my window
The tiles don't live here anymore
My concrete jungle is now rubble
New buildings raised to the floor
My bed is bricks, my windows gone
Hot coffee seems so far away
Showers of tears are all around

My crew are all dead in a day
A dog licks on his humans face
His shattered smile is full of grime
This is my Ukrainian nightmare
And we are running out of time
Transport here are heavy tanks
Taking bodies broken and bare
Everybody is now homeless here
When will somebody care

EVERYONE'S SHAME

Any one broken

Any one caught

Any one left

Everyone fought

No one conquered

No one saw

No one won

In any war

Everyone payed

Everyone lost

Everyone trusted

But at what cost

Nobody rescued

Nobody came

Nobody listened

Everyone's shame

MY ANXIETY MADE ME A SPLIFF

my anxiety made me a spliff
my depression bought me a beer
my anger got me some ketamine
is that what you wanted to hear
my frustration found me some coke
my rage sold me some crack
my temptation brought me copious sex
i dont want to ever go back
my boredom sought out mushrooms
my suicide laced me with heroin
my loss told me to chain smoke
and put my mental health in the bin
my curiosity stole me some fun
my ignorance left me my bliss
my whole persona is broken in two
and death has left me a kiss

UNDER THE RUBBLE

Under the rubble there lies a child
Who is no longer weak, who is no longer mild
This could be a girl, it could be a boy
They were once their father and mothers joy
They once ran free along the streets
You once could hear their patter of feet
They once sang songs with gracious words
In a voice so beautiful, i once heard
Their big brown eyes would light up a room
Their laughter took away all of the gloom
They danced with friends, they danced with others
And warmed the hearts of one another
Their dreams were big and bright and bold
They dreamed of adventures to behold
They heard the stories of their past
And when they hugged it was their last
Under the rubble, they're not the only one
That child is missing, that child is gone
There is no laughter, there's only tears
It's been the same hell for 75 years
Their big brown eyes won't open again
Their laughter will never sooth their friends
Their rubble has buried all their dreams
But i will always hear their screams

There's thousands more that are buried deep
Their mothers dig and pray and weep
Their Papa sobbed and asks "but why"
"Did you kill take my child, who was only 5"
What was their future, what was their name
Their right to life is a valid claim
Under the rubble, buried deep in the floor
That child is mine and that child is yours

I'M QUEER

im queer

youre what

im queer

im here

youre not

IM QUEER

you hear

and im not guna disappear

and youll always here

my voice

my choice

and my abiltity to cheer

the queers

the queers

we're always so near

to the knuckle

and we struggle

THEY BROUGHT ME FLOWERS

they brought me flowers to my grave
they brought me flowers so id be brave
they brought me flowers to make me glad
they brought me flowers now i feel sad
they brought me flowers to hide my pain
they brought me flowers out of the rain
they brought me flowers to hush my heart
they brought me flowers to play my part
they brought me flowers to cloud my mind
they brought me flowers for me to find
they brought me flowers to give me hope
they brought me flowers so i dont mope
they brought me flowers to give me light
they brought me flowers to help me fight
they brought me flowers coz im not there
they brought me flowers to show they care

Jackie Montague lives in Ipswich and has a car. Most recently, she's headlined at Word Habit, Sudbury, Norwich Last Poet Standing, and East Anglian Story Telling Festival. With many open mics along the way.

As part of Instant Vortex Plus Live Art Happening, she compered and performed a dark and shitty King Lear adaptation at Colchester Arts Centre. For this she wore a ruff. But don't let this seemingly highbrow vibe fool you! She will always love the filthy, punky, campy, trashy stuff the best. Indeed, as a teenager, Jackie was the support act for Lily Savage back in 89 performing a lip syncing turn as Sonia, you know. You'll never stop me from loving you. Sigh...Jackie has obviously dined out on this true story ever since.

jackieandsadie@hotmail.com

@brainwavesarebetterthanperms

ACT 1: THE LOVE TEST (OR Whatever in Love Means OR Nothing Will Come of Nothing)

Introduction: An extract of a shitty and dark King Leery inspired piece exploring the double ended dildo of A Queen's Death and New King carve up via Jimmy Savile.

Turn the telly up
For it's always quite the shit show
Hitting the fans
loving more than eyesight
more than space and liberty
There you can see it. Set in stone. Carved up hard.
Dragged through the streets of Swinging London
Again!

May prick nor purse never fail you
May prick nor purse never fail you
May prick nor purse never fail you
Can you smell the piss?

Trickling down
It's fruity swagger haze upon the breath.
The Dis infected dribble of the born to rile brigade

(Jackie Sings)

We'll Meet Again fucking in alleys without looking up
Show us your knickers!
Born to sweet submission
No fur coats for your knees:
The self-helpless gob stoppers
Still suffering from centuriessss of family

Passing through flabby ghosts
Passing over the dispossessed
Passing Out through flavoured enemas
Licking the anus of the sunken land
Bones forever digging up living off the crumbs
they all eat it all FIRST
and still they gorged on the sweet young fruit
their slippery tentacles reaching, picking it off

Fuck this is awful
Do you ever get the feeling you've been cheated?
Ridicule is nothing to be scared of
It drips through the cracks as

(Here Jackie re-enacts the 1970s Birdseye pea advert)

Prince Charming peers through the fog

Pea soup goes top of the pops

The smoke and Mirrors Mirrors Mirrors

Mirror Mirror on the wall

Who's the reflection of them all?

(Jackie mimes with a cigar as she does an impression of Jimmy Savile)

Now then now then.

Now then Now then Now then Now then

How's about that then

She's a very busy lady

Stinking old hags

Always on the blag

Just bitter old slags

BETHNAL GREEN GIRL

Introduction: Bethnal Green Girl Shamima Begum is British and should be repatriated. Full stop.

The quality of mercy is stained

Yellowing

Before the eyes

for an eye

and tooth for tooth

slowly sharpening the knives are out

for the pound of flesh

To be savoured, succulent, revenge tastes sweet

Sourly served cold

over the flames

for the righteous

Repatriation?

Confused with

moral absolution

Taking the 'tough decisions'

and wrapping them up in neatly

You don't have to agree to see she's

NOW a

Political liability

Too much Too Much Too Much Too Much
In a desert of borders and Brexit
And swarms and the boring
Consequences
of wars
and colonialism
YAWN

And fingers still swirling in long ancient crusting
pies of power.

Licking the spoon
feeding children
bites the hands that feeds them.

Mean . Pin pricks.
Irritate and burn
and swell
and throb with anger.
A blood blister. Scratch. Pus. Scabs

Stripped citizen ship
Sails off into a sunset
Spun gold by legal fictions
And home secretary discretion.
Dis excretion
Dis excrement

Home?
There's no place like it.

DIRTY WEEKEND DREAM

*Introduction : A Dirty Weekend Dream of Nostalgia
and sex. Inspired by the ruins of the Overstrand Hotel,
Norfolk (which she has never visited) and the
Cemetery, Ipswich (which she has visited.)*

Satin stroking
tongues caressing in waves
Gin slinging off the shoulder blades
over the top room service.

Did the earth move for you, darling?
Make or breakfast and
full board
pushing penetrating devouring licking its salty fingers
and roaring in pleasure
grinding crumbling morsels,
Her story never knowingly misquoted.
Sand paper towels and navy blue lips do not disturb
fine dining.
For there is still a Jurassic spark and worse things
happened at sea battening down the hatches
Flotsum and jizzum
In and out and up and down
giving a wide berth only to the dumb water
drowning in Mulligatawny soup.
Slurping. Serving
The Etiquette.

A SITCUM

Introduction: A SitCum Breathing life back into Jackie's favourite genres and actresses. They definitely don't make them like that anymore!

Who Gets The House?: A Smeggy rock opera in 5 bowel movements

Lady Inertia: Joan Sims

Miss Havishspam: Hattie Jacques

Madame De Ferret: Yootha Joyce

Overbite

Lady Inertia was wasting away.

But her correspondence with Miss Havishspam

and Madame De Ferret kept her going,

in between hourly bouts of masturbation

in sheets that hadn't been changed

for moths, even.

The irony had amused all three women, who were

really down on their uppers:

Discarded.

Dumped.

Beautifully bitter.

They swam in the bile and sucked from its breast.

It kept them going.

That acidic thrill.

As they discussed at length,

How Diana Dors proved this could all be done

as the

haggy Mrs Wickens in The Amazing Mr Blunden

in 1791.

A great turn.

An unforgettable decent in to playing ugly.

Parts of character.

CUE:

SONG:

"So Brave ..."

(All 3 eye roll as one)

Milton Keynes UK
Ingram Content Group UK Ltd.
UKHW021533080424
440673UK00007B/69